OUR GRANDMOTHER

By
Tona Whaley

AuthorHouse™
1663 Liberty Drive
Bloomington, IN 47403
www.authorhouse.com
Phone: 833-262-8899

This book is printed on acid-free paper.

ISBN: 978-1-6655-3318-8 (sc)
ISBN: 978-1-6655-3319-5 (e)

Print information available on the last page.

Published by AuthorHouse 02/01/2022

authorHOUSE®

Our Grandmother is so nice to us; she lets us do so many fun things.

My Grandmother lets me eat all the fruit I want. I eat an apple.

I eat a banana.

I eat a pear.

The grapes are yummy.

Watermelon is my favorite fruit, I can't wait to eat it.

Grandmother lets me enjoy sticks in every way.

I play drums with sticks.

After I eat I pick my teeth with a little toothpick stick.

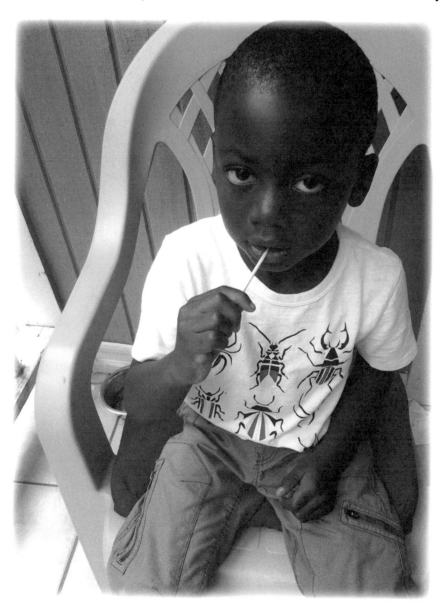

 I cook marshmallows on a stick, but I think the fire is lost.

I enjoy playing with a big stick at the park, this one is heavy.

We love to ride!

I love to ride in the red wagon, it is so much fun when I am getting pulled all around.

I love to go horse back riding, it makes me feel taller than everyone on the ground.

I love riding my bike on the bike trail, it is good exercise for my health.

I love riding my bike out back. Sometimes I ride my friends too, they keep coming back for more rides.

I enjoy horseback riding too, it is a wonderful connection with the horse, and it makes me feel big and brave.

When I come over to Grandmother's house, I have fun.

First, I go get Alley the Alligator. He is so big but I can still carry him on my back.

After playing with Alley the Alligator, I will draw a picture for my mother.

Next, I go to the drums to make a lot of noise. Oh boy! I love these drums. Grandmother says it is too noisy but she still let me play them.

Grandmother took me to get lunch, and I am happy because playing made me hungry.

After lunch, I think I will lie down and take a nice long nap until mommy comes to pick me up.

We like coming to Grandmother's house after school.

Grandmother helps us with our homework and gives us good snacks.

After I do my homework, I will play games on the computer.

I am trying to hurry because I am so hungry for Grandmother's tasty cake.

Yay, it is snack time and we are ready for Grandmother's good tasting cake. Yummy Yummy!

Grandmother made my day when she gave me an airplane ticket.

Grandmother and I went to L.A. to visit my awesome Uncle Chazz. This was so special because Grandmother and I had never flown on an airplane before. We were a little nervous. Grandmother brought me lunch while we waited for the plane to come. We got on the airplane and Grandmother let me sit by the window. Grandmother said that I was brave. The ride was plenty to take in. Taking off was somewhat scary, but once we were in the air, I felt more settled. Looking out at the clouds and seeing how small everything looked was an amazing treat.

Next, we went walking and saw a really really big chair. It was the biggest chair we had ever seen. Grandmother and I took a picture in it.

I also took a picture in a palm tree by myself.

And after that, Grandmother and I enjoyed eating some flavored ice. Grandmother like papaya and I like blue raspberry.

Next, we went beach walking together. My Uncle missed all of the fun because he had to work. Grandmother said that we should head back. I did not want to leave the beach water, I loved it. It felt warm to my feet. Grandmother loved it too, and she also enjoyed collecting seashells.

My Uncle Chazz came to pick Grandmother and Me up. Grandmother was walking slow because she was hot and tired. My uncle and I held hands and walked together to the apartment building. He said that we would all get some rest and enjoy the beach tomorrow. Grandmother and I could not wait because we missed having my uncle do fun things with us.

South Carolina here we come!

We are visiting our Grandmother's Grandma's house.

My sister and I enjoyed the train ride. It was a new experience for us. We had never ridden on a train before. Upon arrival at Grandmother's Grandma's house, all of her cats were waiting to welcome us. We freshened up, rested, talked to our Grandmother's Grandma for a little while, and went to dinner.

Yummy Yummy Yummy! Grandmother lets us order whatever we want. My sister and I are enjoying this good food. After we are done, we will take a nice walk to the lake with Grandmother.

I enjoy throwing rocks into the water.

My sister enjoys playing in the water with sticks.

I need to get back to the house now because I have a church flea market to go to. I will buy everything that I like. My sister and grandmother did not want to come with me. The church flea market was only outside on the church parking lot. I can do this on my own. The church flea market was fun. I brought cloths, food and some other stuff. It felt good spending my own money on whatever I wanted.

We spent a little more time at Grandmother's Grandma's house and then got back on the train and headed back home. What an amazing trip!

Grandmother goes to church.

Grandmother goes to church a lot; she takes us to church sometimes with her.

When I go with her, I clap my hands

In children's church, my sister and I listen and learn about GOD.

When I go to church with Grandmother, I lay my head on the back of the chair and listen.

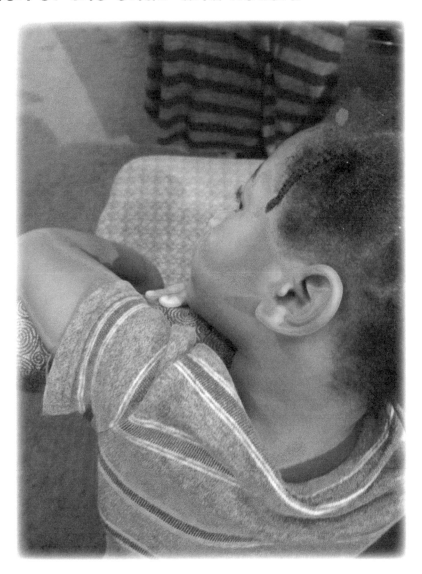

And then I fall asleep.

Grandmother is the best!

Printed in the United States
by Baker & Taylor Publisher Services